Gratitude through Trials

Redeemed and Loved

LAURIE KIRBY

GRATITUDE THROUGH TRIALS

Redeemed and Loved

Copyright © 2017. Laurie Kirby

All Rights Reserved. No part of this publication may be reproduced, distributed, or transmitted in any form or by any means, including photocopying, recording, or other electronic or mechanical methods, without the prior written permission of the publisher, except in the case of brief quotations embodied in critical reviews and certain other noncommercial uses permitted by copyright law.

Published by

Transcendent Publishing
PO Box 66202
St. Pete Beach, FL 33706
www.transcendentpublishing.com

Cover Art Photography by Sarah Kirby

First Edition January 2017
Second Edition August 2018

ISBN-13: 978-1-7320764-1-9

Library of Congress Control Number: 2017932147

Printed in the United States of America.

DEDICATION

This book is my testimony, written in dedication to God. He has delivered, redeemed and loved me unconditionally, even when I didn't deserve it. To my dear friend, Sharon Chapman, whose encouragement through the years has been immeasurable, and those friends who have patiently waited for me to finish this work of love, I could not have done this without you.

CONTENTS

About Myself 1

Early Years 5

Growing Up 9

Billy 13

Brian 15

Marriage 19

Babies 23

Moving Once Again 29

Divorce 31

Life Alone 35

Tough Times 37

Surgery 41

The Boss 43

Continuing Trouble At Work, And 45

Our Remarriage 45

A Fresh Start 49

Further Surgery 51

Drugs And Infidelity 53

    Side Thoughts/Journaling: 55

Our Pathway Out 59

Surgery Yet Again	61
Through It All, Our God	65
Gratitude	67
My Children	69
Ryan	69
Sarah	69
Kyle	70
My Wish For You	73
Acknowledgements	75

ABOUT MYSELF

When I was young, my family moved a lot. The longest we ever lived anywhere was on our farm in Kentucky for six years. It was 170 acres of beauty with hidden caves, trees, pastureland, a creek, pond and fertile ground. There was never a dull moment living on a farm. It was hard work, but became a wonderland that held this child's wild imagination captive.

Fast forward about 10 years, I was an adult living in California just starting a career with McDonnell Douglas, which later became The Boeing Company. I worked at Boeing for 23+ years, gaining invaluable experience working with a variety of customers, striving for "customer satisfaction" and first-rate quality in all that I did. While at McDonnell Douglas/Boeing, I received Six Employee Recognition Awards for Outstanding Performance with C-17 Human Resources & C-17 Airframe IPT, Three Employee Recognition Awards for Outstanding Performance with C-17 Airframe IPT, Nine Performance Bonuses & Performance Recognition Letters with C-17 Airframe IPT, and C-17 Airframe & Mission Systems—Employee of the Month June 2005.

Moving often as a child made "having roots" and

owning my own home even more important to me. Over the years, I had always loved attending open houses, seeing how other people lived, and picturing how I could renovate a neglected house. That was exciting! I decided to get my license and pursue real estate in 2006. It's been an adventure meeting new people every day, hearing their dreams of owning a home and more importantly, helping them make those dreams come true!

Volunteer Experience & Causes

Sharefest

I've participated in Sharefest through our church outreach program for over eight years now. We provide assistance to people and schools on their homes/buildings with painting, plumbing, gardening, concrete work when they cannot afford these improvements.

Causes I care about:

- Children
- Disaster and Humanitarian Relief
- Animal Abuse

Organizations I support:

- Samaritan's Purse
- World Impact

- Compassion International
- American Cancer Society
- Alzheimer's Association

This book wasn't intended to point fingers, to lay bare our sins and weaknesses, shouting, "Look what she did!!" or "See what he did!" It's instead offered as a glimpse at the powerful, undeniable, living God that made us, and His redeeming grace and love given to us, despite our unworthiness. Many people will read these stories and think, "I would never do anything like that!" or "How could she stay with someone who would do that?!" When you have made a commitment to someone who becomes trapped in the bondage of addiction, you'd be surprised by what you'd do. From my experience, I can assert that drugs are evil. Drugs change a person in unimaginable ways. The person who gets hooked doesn't wake up one morning and decide to become a drug addict. It's a gradual decline that rots the mind and soul. Remember, we are ALL sinners, our righteousness is as filthy rags in the eyes of God. We are all on a level playing field, whether you choose to believe that or not. Our redemption only comes through the blood of Christ.

Looking back on my life, I can see it has been a journey filled with trials that have made me who I am today. It's been a life filled with happiness and, at times, extreme anguish.

LAURIE KIRBY

EARLY YEARS

Stepping back in time, I was born on March 3, 1964 in Wentzville, Missouri. Over the next six years, we moved from state to state, every three to six months. My dad always seemed to think life would be better in a new location; however, the contentment he sought was ever elusive. As an adult and a Christian, I realize he was searching for something to fill the emptiness inside. If he had turned his life over to Christ, our lives might have been different. Yet everyone's journey is unique, with unforeseen circumstances often beyond our control. In Philippians 4:11-13, the Apostle Paul says, "[11] I am not saying this because I am in need, for I have learned to be content whatever the circumstances. [12] I know what it is to be in need, and I know what it is to have plenty. I have learned the secret of being content in any and every situation, whether well fed or hungry, whether living in plenty or in want. [13] I can do all this through Him who gives me strength."

When I was six, we moved back to Kentucky, one of the many states we had lived in, and where our grandfather owned a farm. We stayed for about a year then moved to Indiana. After nine months, it was back to Kentucky and the farm. Our grandfather and grandmother had passed away and left half of the farm to my uncle (my dad's brother) and the other half to my father. In total, there were 170 acres. We loved the farm, even though it required hard physical labor, and had no modern amenities other than electricity. I was eight or nine years old before we had running water in the house. We had to use the outhouse until my dad finally built a bathroom, which was completed when I was around eleven years old. It's no wonder I love showers! You learn to appreciate the simple things most take for granted, like indoor running water, a bathroom (no more looking for "critters" before you sat down!) and a real washing machine. My mother would do our laundry over a washboard and washtub until we bought a wringer-washing machine. Summers meant hoeing three acres of tobacco, an acre garden and hauling in hay. This was on top of the daily chores of milking the cows, feeding the cows and chickens, collecting the eggs, cleaning the barn and chicken coop, mending fences and a variety of other tasks. In our spare time, we spent hours exploring our farm, with small caves, streams, a creek, a pond and lots of woods. My brother Stoney and I would go fishing whenever we could. If we would get into a fight, our way of making up would be to go fishing together. Stoney would grab the fishing poles and I would dig the worms. Sometimes we would sneak some salt pork out of the fridge. The fish loved that!

School started in August and we usually had vacation in May unless we had to make up snow days. Our mornings before school consisted of getting up at 4:00 a.m. to milk and feed the cows, eat breakfast then walk a mile to the bus pickup. When it was raining, mom would put bread wrappers over our shoes to keep our shoes dry and clean. The bus ride was about an hour long as the driver picked up kids on the route to school. During the bus ride, my friend Debbie and I would share our dreams of what we'd do when we grew up. I wanted to stay on the farm, raise horses and become a veterinarian. I would also tell her stories from our many moves from state to state.

When my father was laid off, we had no income. He tried driving a coal truck but that didn't last long. For a couple of years, my dad fell into a depression. He slept a lot, stopped interacting with us, and was more irritable than usual. Finally, my mother had enough and told him he had to get a job. He found work in Nashville and would come home on the weekends, staying in a motel during the week. That winter, we had one of the worst storms in years. An ice storm, followed by 23 inches of snow. We didn't go to school from the first of December until February. Our dad couldn't get down to see us for over two weeks. We were running out of food so Stoney and I went hunting. Mom would offer us words of comfort. I would play my guitar and sing. We had our own little "hoe-down"!

One day, my brother and I were so bored we took off the legs on our Mom's ironing board, and used it to race down the hills in the snow. We were having a blast! Mom came out to watch us and was smiling and laughing at our antics, until she realized what we using for our sled! The expression on her face was priceless! But in all fairness, she wasn't all that upset. We replaced the legs once we were done. So many good memories, even though we didn't have much by way of worldly means.

We would sit around the dining room table at lunch and Mom would tell us stories of her childhood, the war, and her life before marrying our dad. She was a great storyteller; so animated! We were spellbound by her every word!

GROWING UP

Mom was a Christian, always reading her Bible and praying. I don't remember a time that I didn't believe in Jesus. I was saved when I was ten years old and baptized in McQuady's pond. We couldn't attend church often, but it was special when we could.

When I was 13, Dad decided to sell his half of the farm. We were heartbroken, didn't want to move. We wound up moving to Tennessee, a stay that only lasted about eight months. We then moved to Garden Grove, California and that only lasted three months. We returned to Kentucky and lived on my uncle's side of the farm. Again, that didn't last. My sister married when she was 17, then during that summer, we trekked off to California. My sister, a young newlywed, was devastated. We lived in California for about ten or 11 months, at which time Stoney and I went to high school at North High in Torrance. I joined Anza Avenue Baptist Church in Torrance. If I wasn't at school, I was at church. Around May, we were on the move again, but this time to Kansas. Dad landed a job at Boeing, while Mom and I worked at a nursing home (she was the cook and I was her assistant/aide). After three months, we had enough money to rent an apartment in Rose Hill,

Kansas. Stoney and I were now students at Rose Hill High School. In time we made friends, I joined Track and Field and threw shot and disc. I wasn't very good but it was a lot of fun cheering on our teammates and going to meets. In between sports, I worked at the nursing home in Rose Hill as a nurse's aide. After school, I would be there from 5 p.m. to 11:00 p.m. I would then come home, do my homework/study, then was off to bed. During the summer, I worked as much as I could, sometimes even taking double-shifts. It was physically demanding, but very rewarding. The elderly people were so grateful that I would help them with a smile. They'd often entertain me with the jokes they'd tell. During my junior year, I quit my job at the nursing home and went to work at Kmart in Wichita. Some of my friends from school worked there also so that made the job fun. I was quickly promoted from the Layaway Room to Checkout, then to Checkout Supervisor. Life was good.

I had many friends at school. Most would tell me, "Laurie, you're so nice, you never seem to do anything wrong." For some reason, perhaps due to my immaturity as a young Christian, when invited to a bonfire party on a Friday night, I decided to go and show them I could be "bad." I was offered a beer and as the night wore on, drank that and more. Only by the grace of God did I arrive home because I honestly don't know how I stayed on the road. Mind you, my dad was in the hospital recovering from gallbladder surgery, so my brother Stoney, my mom and my sister Karen, who was visiting from Kentucky, were home. I thought I had gone to bed but I didn't. I stayed up for over an hour babbling. My poor mom and sister, who sat through all my nonsense. The next morning, we visited my dad in the hospital. I had drunk so much that the alcohol was coming out of my pores, even though I had taken a shower. I gave my dad a quick kiss then backed away, fearing he'd detect the smell. This was my first experience with drinking. I can't say I never drank again. I continued to attend parties where alcohol was served. If I had been involved with a good church and reading my Bible more faithfully, I could avoided those temptations, and not have been so desperate to fit in. 1 Corinthians 10:13 says, "No temptation has overtaken you except what is common to mankind. And God is faithful; he will not let you be tempted beyond what you can bear. But when you are tempted, he will also provide a way out so that you can endure it."

My parents were worried I would start drinking too much. In June of '81 my parents decided to return to California. I wanted to stay in Kansas so I could graduate with my class but my dad wouldn't agree. I only needed one semester to graduate since I had extra credits. My friend's parents said I could stay with them but my dad still wouldn't allow it. I was both angry and sad. We moved to Port Hueneme, California, where Dad took a job as a mechanic for a Toyota dealership with one of my mother's brothers. I enrolled at Port Hueneme High School. After two months, Dad was again hired by Northrop so we moved to Hawthorne, California. By this time, I was so disgusted with all the upheaval, I decided to take the California High School Proficiency Test (basically a GED) and passed. I started working full time at age sixteen.

BILLY

Since we were in Hawthorne, close to Anza Baptist Church, which was my previous church, I began attending their services when I was seventeen. A friend from church introduced me to his best friend, Billy, and we started dating. We took a road trip to San Luis Obispo to visit his grandmother, spent a day at the Renaissance Faire, went hiking, and more. In the process, we fell in love. He wanted to get married. Thank goodness, I had enough sense to say we should wait. After all, I was only 17 and he was nineteen.

A few months later we broke up, and he went back to seeing his previous girlfriend. During those few weeks, I dated a couple of guys, but they were nothing to write home about. Billy called and we began spending time together. On my 18th birthday, he sent me a baker's dozen of red roses. Then, inexplicably, he began to avoid me. It wasn't until later that I learned he had been using drugs. We broke up in July of 1982.

LAURIE KIRBY

BRIAN

My longtime friend had broken up with her boyfriend Brian and was dating someone else. She thought I might like Brian, now that he was available. In September of 1982, he called, and asked me to go to a movie with him. I said sure. I had known Brian since I was 14, but he was my friend's boyfriend. After that first date, Billy called. His parents were having a party and he said he missed me. I went to the party to see if I still had feelings for him. On my way home, on the 91 Freeway, my car (the one my dad usually let me drive) blew a rod. Mind you, this was during the time the Hillside Strangler was murdering young women, so I was terrified. It was around midnight, and I coasted over to the shoulder and got out of the car. I saw houses on the other side of the wall so I went down the embankment to try to climb over the wall. What can I say; I was scare out of my wits! I couldn't just jump over a 12-foot-high wall!

As I was coming up the embankment back to the car, a police car pulled up and the officers asked what I was doing. I told them I blew the engine. One of the policemen asked me why I didn't use the callbox. I didn't see one. He pointed up ahead about 50 feet. I went to the callbox and the police took off! I told the operator they were leaving and she couldn't believe it. They are required to wait until you get safely back inside your car. Billy and his best friend Eric came to get me; Billy had AAA and called a tow truck. They towed the car to my house in Hawthorne. My dad was furious that I had taken the car and destroyed the engine. After Billy left, my mom said Brian had called. She told Brian I was seeing Billy. I asked her why she didn't take a message. She wanted me to date Brian instead of Billy! I assured her Billy and I weren't serious. I called Brian the next day. For some reason, after one date, he thought I was his girlfriend. I was angry that he would make that assumption, but I also found it endearing. We were a couple from that day forward.

My life was never the same. We were inseparable, and enjoyed a number of activities together. Brian took me dirt-biking, which I had never done before. He would show off his skills by speeding down the dirt path in the desert, doing a wheelie. When I showed an interest in learning, he taught me to ride. Needless to say, his Yamaha YZ400 was so heavy, if I didn't go fast enough in the sand, I would crash! But that didn't stop me! In time, he bought me my own, smaller dirt bike.

After Brian and I dated for seven months, my parents announced they were moving to Tennessee. I decided not to go. I had just turned 19 and was living in a studio apartment. In April, the day they left, my dad said he was taking his two vehicles. I asked him what I would drive to work, and he asked me to come with them. I told him again I wasn't going, so I was without a car. Brian owned a hot rod he had built, a 1965 Chevy

Nova. It had a lot of power. He let me drive it until I could purchase my own car. After about a month of driving it (it had terrible gas mileage!), I bought my first new car, a 1983 Toyota Starlet. It was a five-speed manual, so I had to learn to drive a stick, but the price fit my budget.

***

I had a good job with a startup company called CAS Worldcom, owned by two brothers. I learned so much from them. They had a "new" computer from Digital (in 1982 that was high-tech!). I became proficient at using its software, and they expanded my duties to include accounting, making marketing materials, and customer service. I stayed there for two years but the joint venture the company had with Time Warner did not pan out, so CAS went out of business. I then worked for a coin-operated laundry equipment company as a secretary in their marketing department.

LAURIE KIRBY

MARRIAGE

My relationship with Brian had become a challenge. Brian would say he was coming to see me but then would not show up. He would call the next day and apologize and be there after work the next day. I knew he was drinking and figured he would grow out of it. He did drink quite frequently (or at least, I thought it was drinking). I started to feel as this was a one-sided relationship, but didn't want to tell my parents. I knew what their advice would be. When his erratic behavior continued, I decided not to see him again. He knew this, and proposed. I said he had to change and he promised he would. I'm the girl who looked at life with rose-colored glasses. I thought once we got married he would stop drinking and we would live happily ever after. I could not have been more wrong!

Brian proposed in April 1984 and we were married July 28, 1984. I was 20 years old, Brian twenty-five. It was a small outdoor wedding. My parents couldn't be there because my dad had suffered a heart attack about a month, before so he couldn't travel. My uncle gave me away. After the wedding and reception, instead of going to our room at the Disneyland Hotel, Brian wanted to stop by his best friend's, also the best man, for a few more drinks. I wasn't too happy about it but agreed. He drank two bottles of champagne and a couple of beers and as we were leaving for the hotel, Brian threw up all over the driveway. I guess this should have been a wake-up call, the beginning of our next 26 years together. We arrived at the hotel, showered and had a nice dinner on our balcony, with a view of the fireworks display at Disneyland. Brian apologized for his earlier behavior and promised to be a good husband. The next day, we went with my brother and sister to Six Flags Magic Mountain, and had a great time. We didn't have much money so that was the extent of our honeymoon. The next day we both returned to work.

Brian did change some, but not as much as I would have liked. On Fridays after work, Brian often didn't come home, showing up later on Saturday. He always had an excuse, and some of his check would be missing. We would make plans with friends and cancel them, because no one could locate Brian.

***

In April of 1985, Brian and I drove to my parents' home in Tennessee. Brian's family called us there to say his mom, Nancy, was in the hospital after having a heart attack, and wasn't expected to survive. We immediately left, but it took us two days to reach the hospital, and she had already passed. This was a profound loss for Brian's family. Nancy was the "glue" that held them together. I think Brian had a difficult time handling the death of his mother, although he didn't get emotional or want to talk about it. Our lives continued much as they had been. I was always on edge wondering if my husband was coming home, or all his money was spent.

In January of 1986, I submitted a job application at McDonnell Douglas. I didn't hear anything for a few months then at the end of May 1986, I received a call from Human Resources. They wanted to interview me for an HR position. I met with the hiring manager and he offered me the job. I gave my two weeks' notice and on June 4, 1986 began working at McDonnell Douglas. I was excited about the excellent benefits and opportunity for advancement. After I'd worked there a few months, Brian and I decided to buy a house. We put in a bid on a little two-bedroom house (598 sq. ft.) in Long Beach. While we were waiting for escrow to close, I found out Brian wasn't just drinking, he was using drugs. I was devastated. I was so naive. I asked God to give me strength to get through this and for Brian to stop using.

LAURIE KIRBY

BABIES

We decided to buy the house, and gave notice at our apartment. Brian's oldest brother let us stay at his place for a month while we were in escrow, to save money for furniture and the expenses we'd have when we closed. While we were there, some nights Brian wouldn't come home. I was uncomfortable at his brother's house by myself. Since we still had a few nights paid at our apartment, I slept there when he was gone. I would lie on the bare floor (we had no furniture), with my coat over me, in tears, asking God for help.

We closed escrow around February 1987. You would think when buying our first house, with both of us having good jobs and some "desert toys," life would be good. We had been trying to have a baby but with no success. My gynecologist sent me to a specialist. The infertility doctor put me on Clomed, a fertility medication, since I didn't ovulate correctly. After two months of taking Clomed, I conceived. I was happy beyond words. Brian seemed genuinely happy, too, since he wanted a large family, and was one of nine children. But the realization that he was going to be a father put Brian in a tailspin. He started using drugs more frequently.

I was only pregnant about three months when my brother Stoney came to live with us. This was probably not the smartest move on my part but I didn't realize my brother also had a problem with drinking and drugs. Brian found Stoney a position at his job but it wasn't long before they went to the Union Hall and complained that the work should have been under union control. Needless to say, the site was shut down and Brian and Stoney were out of work. This made our situation even worse. Finally, I asked my brother to move out.

About a year later, Stoney renewed his commitment to Christ and stopped using drugs. Although he still drank, this was an answer to prayer. He was about to face a life-long test of faith; a battle with cancer. I am happy to report my brother is now 54 years old and still continuing this race called life.

By this time, I was nine months pregnant. I didn't know if Brian would be there with me when I went into labor and I was scared. I prayed and cried so much, pouring my heart out to God. When I did go into labor, only by God's grace was Brian there to take me to the hospital. I was in labor 36 hours. The baby wanted to come out sunny-side up, which means both shoulders were trying to exit the birth canal. The baby's heartrate along with mine started to drop. The doctor said he would try the vacuum extractor but if that didn't work, I would need a C-section. I was determined to have "natural childbirth," but as you can imagine, by now I wanted some drugs! Of course, the nurses said too late. The extractor worked after a few more pushes, and our beautiful baby boy was placed in my arms. Ryan Keith

Kirby was 7 lbs. 11 ½ oz., the most precious gift God had blessed me with. I couldn't believe he was my baby. I never wanted to put him down. I was totally in love with my beloved son.

***

After the birth of Ryan, and with no job, Brian sank deeper into drug addiction. I asked my oldest brother Dan for advice. He suggested I join him in the state of Washington, where he was working. He would pay for my airfare and I could stay a few days at his apartment. Ryan was only six weeks old, and I took Dan up on the offer. I did a lot of soul searching, praying, crying, and more praying. I kept asking myself, "Why would someone resort to drugs when God has given him such a gift?" I had to decide whether or not to stay with Brian, and if so, what steps to take to get him help. The day I returned home, my flight didn't arrive in LAX until 11:00 p.m. and Brian had said he'd pick us up. I waited for an hour, but Brian was a no-show. I ended up calling my friend and she came to get us. When we arrived home, we found him passed out in his truck in the back of the house. Inside the house, I found the baby crib dismantled, foil tacked up the wall by the TV, with dirty dishes and clothes strewn everywhere.

The next morning, I told Brian he had to get help or I was leaving. He agreed to go to outpatient treatment. I would attend meetings with him while my mother watched Ryan. (My parents had come back to California about a year earlier.) After a few weeks, I didn't notice any improvements in Brian's behavior. In fact, he would use, go to class, and make a game of convincing the counselor he was sober. I told him I wouldn't take any more time away from Ryan doing this since he wasn't serious. Because Brian wasn't working, and my salary wasn't enough to pay the mortgage and household expenses, we had to put our house up for sale. It sold in July of 1988. I separated from Brian and moved into a one-bedroom apartment. My mother baby-sat Ryan while I worked.

My days all ran together as I got up very early in the mornings, dropped Ryan off at Mom's then headed off to work. Some nights, Brian would sit under my bedroom window crying, vowing to never use drugs again; he'd beg me to let him in, tell me he missed us, and on and on. This was both infuriating and heart-wrenching at the same time. About six months later, my mom said she couldn't watch Ryan anymore (she was exhibiting early signs of Alzheimer's). I found a woman near us who operated a daycare. After a couple of weeks, I noticed Ryan was terrified of her in the morning when I dropped him off. Then one day I notice his scrotum was rubbed raw on one side. I asked her about it and she said he was asleep in the walker a long time that day. I was furious! I left that sitter and found another daycare. After a couple of days of finding Ryan with spit-up plastered to his head, I decided to surprise her on my lunch break. She was feeding all the kids with the same spoon! I went back to my desk crying, asking God to bring me someone I could trust with my baby. The next day, when I picked Ryan up, he had a bruise over his eye. I questioned her and her response was, "I don't know, he's been in the crib all day." I took him home and never brought him back. At work, a fellow employee had raved about her babysitter Cathy. I met with her and discovered she was the next best thing to being with my own children, just as the girl at work had said. Her home was clean, she fed the kids healthy food, they played happily together, and were given structured time. I don't know what I would have done without Cathy. Many mornings I had to be at my desk by 5:00 a.m. and I could drop Ryan off by 4:30 a.m. Of course, he would be asleep, but knowing my child was safe meant the world to me.

***

Brian and I agreed to try again after he promised to stay on the straight and narrow. We were only together about a month before I was pregnant with our second child. Brian was still struggling with his addiction but he seemed more serious about getting sober. He started work at McDonnell Douglas in 1988, and this was a year later. I was due to have the baby in July of 1990; however, it seemed our child was just too comfortable. When he was past two weeks late, due to his size, the doctor thought it best to induce labor. Brian was there with me…at first, but when he heard it may take a while, Brian decided to have dinner down the street. Needless to say, he didn't show up for the birth of our second son. The nurses asked where my husband had gone. What was I supposed to say, "He went to get a fix?" My OB/GYN doctor wasn't on-call that day so a doctor I didn't know delivered Kyle. After my big, beautiful boy (9 lbs., 2 ½ oz.) was born, the doctor didn't wait for the placenta to detach naturally, so he reached up and yanked it out. The entire ordeal was a nightmare. But my baby boy made it all worthwhile. Brian picked me up the next day, and when I brought the baby home, Ryan (our first son) kept saying, "Put it down, mommy!" I explained that this was his brother and he could help care for him. It didn't take long before they were a twosome! Kyle never wanted to be held, was always crawling, always exploring and on the move.

MOVING ONCE AGAIN

When Kyle was nearly six weeks old, we relocated to Pennsylvania. My oldest brother Dan worked for a construction company that would employ Brian so I could stay at home with the boys. We both quit our jobs with McDonnell Douglas and drove to Pennsylvania. In Bridgeville, we rented an old house for our new little family.

Brian did well at first with the construction company. He was learning to build slurry walls. I was home with the boys and loving it. It didn't take Brian long to discover the guys who used drugs and drink. One Friday night, he went with them to a bar. When he didn't come home I began to worry. The Union Steward called to say that Brian was intoxicated and they had put him up in a motel. Brian showed up later that day, and I warned him that if this behavior continued, I would move back to California with the boys and take a position with McDonnell Douglas. I knew he was using drugs again and started making calls to McDonnell Douglas. After ten months in Pennsylvania, I was offered a job. Brian could follow with the furniture and all the boxes I had packed, when his construction job ended in August 1991. The boys and I stayed with my friend in La Mirada (she owned a daycare and watched the boys), until I could find an apartment.

We were there for about three weeks and my friend's husband began making advances. I repeatedly refused him. About a week later, my "friend" said she needed to make a confession to be in good standing with the Lord. She and Brian had an affair a few years back. I was speechless. I thought, *Your husband has been propositioning me, and because you are my best friend, and it's wrong, I've been saying no?* I didn't reply because I didn't want to cause a problem in their marriage. After she told me this news, well, let's just say, Satan has a way of tempting you into things you would never otherwise consider. The next time her husband came onto me, I didn't turn him down. I thought to myself, *I'll show her!* After a week or so, I said I had a confession (much like she had said to me, but without mentioning God), and revealed my affair with her husband. How did that feel?

That night, I tried to sleep, but I knew what I had done was wrong. God wasn't going to give me peace until I told my friend how deeply sorry I was, and I did feel remorse. I felt sick to my stomach. Vengeance is God's, not ours. Needless to say, the boys and I soon moved into an apartment. Brian was again in California but the drugs followed with him; as soon as he was back in town, he scored first then joined us afterwards!

DIVORCE

At that point, we separated. He quickly fell into the drug scene (doing things I don't know about and don't want to know about). He camped under my bedroom window and wept. It's the person dispensing "tough love" who suffers, more than the person who receives it. After a few months, we decided to live together again. Shortly after that, I became pregnant for the third time. At the apartment complex Brian was now the maintenance man. He would be drug-free for about three months, have a slipup, then be good for a few weeks, and on it would go. When I was about eight months pregnant, he was using heavy drugs continuously. We separated again. When I was in labor, Brian said he would be there but he wasn't. My sister flew in from Kentucky. She said she needed to get away and wanted to spend time with the kids and me, offering to be their nanny. I thought it might work so I agreed.

I gave birth to my daughter Sarah, my third child. She was beautiful and the boys loved her. After a couple of weeks, my sister was unhappy. She called her husband to get her and her son. I was scheduled to go back to work in three weeks and had given up my wonderful babysitter! I called to see if she could take the kids in three weeks but she had made other commitments. A neighbor in our apartment complex said she'd watch my children. I hired her and after a few months, in the spring of 1994, I realized she was high on drugs when in our home.

I asked Brian if we should try to save our marriage and he was all for it. He even offered to take over the responsibilities of the kids. It was the usual three months of good behavior, followed by his relapsing. In early 1996, the drug use made our lives untenable. His "dealer" began dropping off drugs in the alley behind our apartment. I was terrified he might leave meth on the sink counter and the kids would think it was sugar. I filed for divorce, which became final in June, 1996. The day of our divorce decree, when the judge stated, "your marriage is dissolved," my heart felt sliced in half. I could not stop crying. The judge looked at me like I was crazy. I viewed marriage as a covenant before God, believed that it was a commitment for life, so the day it was dissolved I was devastated. I went back to my desk after court, still teary-eyed. But at least I still had my job, I was able to get my wonderful babysitter back, and my children and I were together.

***

The kids and I made the best of it. I didn't have much money but my kids knew I loved them. On the weekends, we were always at the beach or the park or hiking. I don't think they ever felt deprived. Sundays were always church days. We joined Oceanside Christian Fellowship in El Segundo in July 1996. After our previous pastor retired, the pastor replacing him began to harass me. Before my divorce was finalized, he would telephone the house at 11:00 p.m., calling me an ungodly woman for divorcing my husband. I repeatedly explained the circumstances leading to my divorce, and asked that he not call so late. Finally, I'd had enough. I threatened to file a complaint, and the calls stopped.

LAURIE KIRBY

LIFE ALONE

We were happy at Oceanside Christian Fellowship (OCF). The kids would invite their friends to go with us on Sundays. We always seemed be surrounded by children. It was a struggle financially but God always provided gas for the car and money for rent. During the week, the kids and I would cuddle up on the couch and read books, which always included the Children's Bible Stories.

When you are having financial difficulty, remember God's many promises to provide for you. Luke 12:24, "Consider the ravens; they neither sow nor reap, they have neither storehouse nor barn, and yet God feeds them. Of how much more value are you than the birds!" Psalm 81:10, "I am the Lord your God, who brought you out of the land of Egypt. Open your mouth wide and I will fill it." Psalm 34:10, "The young lions suffer want and hunger; but those who seek the lord lack no good thing." Psalm 84:11, "For the Lord God is a sun and shield; the Lord bestows favor and honor. No good thing does he withhold from those who walk uprightly." Matthew 6:31-32, "Therefore, do not be anxious saying, "what shall we eat?" or what shall we drink? Or what shall we wear? For the Gentiles seek after all these things, and your heavenly Father knows that you need them all." Philippians 4:19, "And my God will supply every need of yours according to his riches in glory in Christ Jesus." Matthew 7:11, "If you then, who are evil, know how to give good gifts to your children, how much more will your Heavenly Father who is in Heaven give good things to those who ask him!" Matthew 7:7, "In that day, you will ask nothing of me. Truly, truly, I say to you, whatever you ask of the Father in my name, he will give it to you. Until now, you have asked nothing in my name. Ask and you will receive that your joy maybe full." Romans 8:32, "He who did not spare his own Son, but gave him up for us all, how will he not also with him graciously give us all things?"

When my daughter Sarah was only five months old, she came down with the chicken pox. It quickly turned into pneumonia, and she ran a fever of 104 degrees. I prayed and wept, feeling so alone, vulnerable and helpless. That night, it seemed as if the presence of God entered the room, reassuring me that everything would be all right. The next morning, Sarah was better. Her sweet, little face peeked out at me through her crib with the biggest grin. No one can tell me there isn't a God. God was present with me and my children that night. He gave me the encouragement I needed to continue.

In 1997, my sister, her husband and son relocated to California. With my help, Ken was hired at Boeing. A few days after my sister's family arrived in California, my oldest brother Dan paid for me and the kids to fly to Boston where he lived. We stayed for a week and had a great time. That was our first vacation. The kids were so well behaved on the airplane. When we returned home, we decided to rent a house. We found a cute two-bedroom in a good area of Long Beach.

TOUGH TIMES

Brian was still active in the kids' lives. As long as he was sober, I would let him spend time with them. We would schedule time at a park or spend the day together. In January 1998, my dad was living in Kentucky. Mom was in a nursing home because her dementia had progressed. He was also having health issues. I suggested he move back to California so we could provide the care he needed.

Finally, towards the end of the summer of 1998, my oldest brother Dan and I went to Kentucky to bring Dad and Mom back to California. I found a retirement apartment complex in Long Beach where Dad could rent a place, with a nursing home right next door for Mom. Dad would visit us weekly with Mom. He was very sad and missed Mom being at home with him. Mom now didn't speak or recognize us. Dad passed away in September of 1999 and Mom followed in April of 2000. Those months were rough. I had bought a house in July, 1999 in Lakewood. Dad co-signed with me, and planned to move in with me. I thought if he could spend time with the kids, maybe he would be happier. He never had the chance.

I was at home for a few months, recovering from carpal tunnel surgery. Worker's Comp delayed my checks and at one point, I didn't receive a check for an entire month! My cupboards were literally bare, and the mortgage payment was late. After I returned to work, a secretary there asked to rent a room from me. She had separated from her drug-addicted, suicidal husband. I offered her a room for $500 a month. Wow, what a mistake! The first month rent was due, she asked, 'Do you really need it?' Why, yes, I do!! I have three children to feed and a mortgage to pay. She wouldn't clean up after herself, nor would she pitch in with household chores. One day the kids and I came home and discovered her husband on the couch. I flipped out and demanded he leave. If I was going to have an addict in my house, it would be my ex-husband! I also gave her notice. I wasn't willing to jeopardize my children's safety for any reason; the extra income wasn't worth the price.

I decided to sell my house, and closed escrow within a month and a half. I had looked for a house to rent and could not find anything suitable. I submitted a rental application to an older man, Mr. Taylor, and was told he would get back to me. I asked God for guidance. The day before we had to leave our current house, Mr. Taylor called and said we could rent his! God's timing is perfect. This was a test of faith!

We settled into our new home and life was good. My job, on the other hand, was not. For years my boss made covert advances, but that year he pointedly asked me for sex. He could be very understanding when I asked for time off due to personal concerns. But then again, did he have an ulterior motive all along? Other times, he could be very cruel, hurling insults and making unfounded accusations. Some of the engineers in our group would ask, "How do you continue to work for him?" I think my boss (I won't mention his name) sought out my company since I'm "motherly" and willing to listen (sometimes I felt like my group's psychologist!). There was a constant like/dislike tug of war between us. He didn't have a good relationship with his wife and would tell me about it (too much information!). But I have to wonder if his marriage was destroyed by his unfaithfulness, addiction to porn, and other sexual indiscretions. Some days, he would be in such a foul mood that nothing I did was good enough.

LAURIE KIRBY

SURGERY

I had been in a lot of pain, not only emotionally but physically. My neck felt as hard as a rock, and shooting pain ran down my shoulder and back. My right hand was swollen and turning a dark red, and my nail beds were blue. My right arm and elbow were swollen and painful as well. I was afraid to go to the Dispensary because my boss was so unpredictable, but the pain was so debilitating that I couldn't sleep and typing was torture. I finally mustered the courage to get medical attention.

When the doctor saw my right hand, he thought it was Raynaud's Disease (thank God it wasn't). They decided to send me to a specialist, who diagnosed it as a severe case of carpel tunnel. Shortly after that surgery, they sent me to another doctor. I had to undergo radial tunnel release (my right nerve was so inflamed the doctor said he had never seen one so huge and swollen), epicondyle release (this is the muscle that attaches to the elbow bone) and a second carpel tunnel release on the right hand. You would think my boss would have been more understanding. Instead, he asked if I could type his spreadsheet for one of his MBA classes! I explained that my right arm was in a sling and half of my hand was in a soft-cast. He said I could use my left hand. I depended on my paycheck, and to avoid his verbal abuse, I agreed. After I worked another six months, the doctor had to perform carpal tunnel surgery on my left hand. I was on disability for three months.

My boss wanted me at my desk at all times. I would wait until he went to a meeting and transfer my phone just to use the restroom. As soon as I did, he would call. When my co-worker answered, he'd ask, "Where's Laurie?" She'd reply, "She had to use the ladies' room. Can I help you with something?" His answer was usually no. I would call back as soon as I returned only to find it was a task my co-worker could have done. No breaks allowed, no proper ergonomic equipment, with unexpected outbursts; the stress took its toll on my body.

THE BOSS

One day at work, I received a call from my daughter Sarah's school saying she wasn't feeling well and needed to go home. I was given approval to leave the office to pick her. Sarah began to get sick more often, and I told her to tough it out. Then, I would feel like a neglectful mother. On one of these occasions, my boss let loose a tirade.

"You have to be here at work. When you aren't, you're worthless to me. You mean nothing. You don't have a degree. If you tried to get another job, do you think you could make the money you do now?" I reminded him that in 1992 when he hired me, I stipulated that my kids' needs came first. He knew I struggled at home and had agreed to those terms. He became enraged at that response. The next day, he was back to his old self and again trying to pursue me. During these trying times, God reminded me that I was precious in His sight, and the comfort I found in knowing gave me the courage to continue.

I continued to call his requests adultery. He would answer, "Can't you just say a few Hail Mary's?" I repeated I wasn't Catholic, I was Evangelical, and what the Bible says is how I live. He would frequently ask me to lunch. I didn't want to go but usually did, because if I didn't, he would not treat me well. Once when I told him I had too much work, he retorted, "I'm the boss and I say you can go." It was like living with Dr. Jekyll and Mr. Hyde.

In December of 2000, we held our year-end Christmas party. My boss was now asking for sex every day. I was so frustrated, overwhelmed, tired, and at my wit's end with his demands, in addition to the physical problems I was having, I just wanted to scream. After the Christmas party, my boss wanted to go to my house for a drink. I told him I was exhausted and just wanted to go to bed. He would not let it go. To my humiliation, sorrow, and in disobedience, despite my love for God, I gave in. I thought, *Maybe if it's just this once, he'll leave me alone.*

Well, it just got worse. Now he wanted it again, and often. I stood my ground. I told him, "No!! Do you know how I feel, now that I've betrayed God, what I believe in? I'm so ashamed. I cry every day and beg God to forgive me!"

One night, I lay face-down on my bedroom floor in tears, praying for God to deliver me from all that had gone wrong in my life. "If Brian and I were still married, and he didn't use drugs, I wouldn't have so much suffering. Please God, help me!!!"

During the Christmas shutdown at work, while I was at home with the kids, Brian called the day after I poured my heart out in prayer. He needed my help. He had so many drugs in his system, he didn't know how much longer he'd live, and he had lost control. He desperately wanted to end his dependency.

CONTINUING TROUBLE AT WORK, AND OUR REMARRIAGE

I turned to our Pastor/Elder, Denny O'Keefe and repeated Brian's fears. His response was, "It just so happens I have a pamphlet from Beacon House in San Pedro on their rehabilitation program. I'll see what it would take to get him in." He called back to describe the program and what Brian's responsibilities would be. Brian entered Beacon House in January of 2001.

I continued to read my Bible and ask for guidance. As I thought about my response to my boss, I was reminded of the Disciple Peter's reaction when asked if he knew Christ. What shame Peter must have felt after he denied His Lord three times!! My guilt and shame were overwhelming. I knew Christ had redeemed me. Peter denied Christ in fear and weakness, the reasons I also betrayed Him. God helps us to overcome our failings and fears. And prayer is our way to find strength in times of trouble.

In my weakest moment, I allowed Satan to devour me. Scriptures say in 1 Peter 5:8, "Be on the alert, because your adversary, the devil, prowls around like a roaring lion, seeking someone to devour." The many problems in my life overcame me when I submitted to my boss's desires. I should have been on my knees in prayer instead of trying to control of a situation I knew was wrong. I overestimated my ability to resist sin. I also underestimated my fear. The fear of losing my job, which provided for my children and myself. The fear of work becoming a living hell if I didn't give in. I should have turned to Jesus.

We experience trials because Jesus has more for us to learn. I realized I needed to rely on Christ to meet my financial needs, and to provide a way of escape from temptation. For most of my life, I've been so hardheaded, thinking I don't need anyone's help. If I can't do it myself, then I'm not worthy of it. This is the sin of pride. Over the course of my life, Christ has shown me over and over the need to be in prayer and yes, ask for help. My pride has stunted my spiritual growth more than I care to admit.

Now in Beacon House, Brian was doing great. The kids and I visited him often. He was in treatment for nearly three months. When he graduated, he asked if he could live with us. I said yes, and it seemed to be just what we needed. He wanted us to remarry but I had to be sure he wouldn't revert back to using. We waited a year and remarried in July 28, 2002 (the same day we first married in 1984).

***

I informed my boss that Brian and I had remarried. He still made suggestive comments, innuendos, and propositions. During this time, a woman with whom I'd had conflict began dating one of the directors at work. Despite my warning that he pursued sex with multiple women, she wouldn't listen. I warned him of her obsessive attraction to any man who showed an interest her. I discouraged their involvement. I asked them not to involve me. Well, you can imagine what happened. She started sending packages and calling him at the office; she even showed up at his son's gated community. The son told her his dad didn't want to see her. The secretary complained about the emails, cards and packages. I told them again to leave me out of it.

My boss left for a business trip and the next day, the director found me, and said, "We need to talk!" He pulled me into my boss's office, demanding I do something. I reminded him of the warnings he chose to ignore. He wasn't happy.

In the meantime, she made several attempts to find a job at Boeing. She was given the position of Security Guard. When the director found out, he had her terminated and escorted out of the plant. She called me in tears, hoping they'd reconsider. I explained that she'd been let go due to her harassment. She filed a complaint with HR. A few days later, she begged for the job, said she needed it for her four children. At hearing this from HR, I gasped, "Four children? She only has one child!" She was claiming my kids!

***

Between my boss's advances and this continuing drama, I was going off the deep end. I asked Brian if he wanted to go to Washington. He said sure! I started applying for jobs and got an offer with the City of Seattle in the Retirement Office, for more pay than what I was making at Boeing. I gave one month's notice. The boss had tears in his eyes when he asked me, "What am I going to do without you?" I repeated his words that I was worthless and that's when the lightbulb went on. There are consequences to what we say.

A FRESH START

At the end of June 2003, we arrived in Washington. My brother Stoney was employed by the City of Seattle in Waste Management. He had been living in a motel for a month or so. When we rented a house, he asked to stay with us until he could find his own place. We agreed. Brian went to the Union hall to find work (which was sporadic) and also took on odd jobs. The kids hated it there. They missed their friends, our church and school. My job at the Retirement Office was so boring, I had to find things to do. After I finished the tasks I'd been given, I didn't know what to do with my time. Needless to say, I was as miserable as the kids. We decided to head back to California. I was rehired with Boeing, on the B-1B program in Long Beach, in December of 2003. We had a five-month break. God had his hand in all of it. We were able to buy a home and moved in three weeks later, on Christmas Eve.

Brian was sent to a job through the Union Hall, near the house at Lakewood High, a company called FTR International. He would remain with that company for 11 years.

LAURIE KIRBY

FURTHER SURGERY

The kids were enjoying their friends and our lives seemed to be going well. Brian had steady work with FTR and I was again employed at Boeing. In June of 2006, I was staying late to finish a project for a large move into another building. The next morning, I woke up and couldn't move my neck, with pain radiating from my neck down through my left arm. I saw the doctor, and he gave me muscle relaxants and prescription Motrin. Through July I attempted to work but had to start taking time off. I was given physical therapy and saw a chiropractor. During physical therapy, they put traction on my neck to stretch it back into place. An MRI showed my C5-C6 vertebrae had herniated and was pinching the nerve.

After months of no relief, the doctor suggested surgery in January of 2007. He told me that if I went back to doing the same repetitive motions, I would be permanently injured. I already had so much nerve damage and scar tissue there wasn't much they could do. I left Boeing in 2009.

DRUGS AND INFIDELITY

From 2006 through 2012, Brian had periodic setbacks, but by 2011, he was using almost daily. He started suffering physically from all the damage to his body and the effects of the drugs. The tension in the house was unbearable. I had to take him to work and pick him up. Towards the end of 2011, he had missed nearly two months of work. I couldn't believe his employers hadn't fired him; it must have been only by God's grace. I was tired all the time. I drew strength from the promise that God won't give you more than you can bear. Philippians 4:13 states, "I can do all this through him who gives me strength." Another verse that helped me through this stressful time was Psalm 119:28, "My soul is weary with sorrow; strengthen me according to your word." And Isaiah 40:29, "He gives strength to the weary and increases the power of the weak." What would I do without God's Word? Trials teach us to rely on Christ and His unfailing strength.

In February of 2012, Brian's employer went out of business. Since he was still using drugs heavily and had no job, this was a perfect opportunity for outpatient rehab. Couple this with the strong support he was receiving from his men's group at church, and we started to see a difference in his behavior (or so I thought). Only God knows the heart. The Bible says in Jeremiah 17:9-10, "The heart is deceitful above all things, and desperately sick; who can understand it? I the Lord search the heart and test the mind, to give every man according to his ways, according to the fruit of his deeds."

In November of 2012, a few days after Thanksgiving, Brian came into my office at home and said he had something to tell me. "What is it?" I asked. He said he might have "caught something" and needed to get checked, that he had unprotected sex with a hooker. My mouth dropped open in disbelief. My answer was, "So what do you want me to do about it?" Our medical insurance had been cancelled when we lost our jobs. I made an appointment with our family doctor, explained the situation and he ran blood and urine tests on us both. All I could think was how selfish Brian was. Didn't he learn in sex education that his having sex with someone is like me having sex with that person as well? Well, the test results were all negative, PRAISE GOD!! Brian expressed how sorry he was and promised to change. Our pastor/elder had been helping Brian through this journey since 2001. Denny O'Keefe had some strong words with Brian about his actions and behavior.

I didn't sleep with Brian for a few months after that episode. I was deeply hurt, felt betrayed and didn't trust him. I started noticing disturbing comments on his Facebook private messages. He had "friended" one of the secretaries from his old place of employment, and insisted they were just friends. Then I noticed he was deleting some of his messages. His phone would ring and when I'd answer it, the person on the other end would hang up. One day, his phone rang, I answered and the caller hung up. A minute later, he received the text, "Oh shit, she picked up." I confronted Brian. He again said they were just friends. I demanded he delete her. He refused. I went onto his Facebook and sent her the private message that I was Brian's wife and didn't appreciate her calling and texting him. Her reply was that she could be his friend if she wanted, and she could even have sex with him if she wanted. It got ugly, and I won't include all that she wrote. I printed out the exchange and handed it to Brian, told him to either delete her number and address and have no more contact with her or he could leave. It was her or me. He again refused to delete her so I did. I told him I wanted to go to marriage counseling. He agreed but never followed through. I emailed the message exchange to Denny. He wrote to Brian and that seemed to have an impact. This all took place in June/July 2013, and the following is an excerpt from my journal on the aftermath of this betrayal:

Side Thoughts/Journaling:

June 12, 2013 at 3:00 a.m. Can't sleep. Thoughts keep running through my mind of why Brian is never satisfied with me. He always seems to be looking for someone else. He hasn't approached me for intimacy in such a long time other than to satisfy himself. I miss being wanted. I'm married but I feel alone. Every day we argue. We don't have the same goals, spiritually and otherwise. He's constantly on the computer. I know he's searching on Facebook for girls, like that Admin from FTR. He sent her the friend request. I don't trust any of the women he worked with at FTR.

You would think any man who truly loved his wife, knowing that his "friend" intimidates his wife, would delete her from his contacts. Not Brian. He gets angry and defensive when I ask him not to communicate with other women, which tells me how little he values me, and it seems he doesn't value our so-called marriage much either. Now he's deleted all his private messages, which tells me he's starting to sneak around again, and that just increases my mistrust. He makes excuses when I need help, but when it's something he shouldn't be doing, he sure finds a way. And tonight, instead of his sleeping on the couch, I asked him to go to bed with me. He got mad and stomped like a two-year-old all the way to the bedroom, as if my bed was a place of punishment.

I have asked him repeatedly for marriage counseling and he says no, I can go by myself. It takes two to make a marriage. The only reason he agreed to go in January was because I was about to throw his ass on the street, when he admitted to unprotected sex, and was afraid he'd caught something. He didn't tell me because he felt guilty or because he might have infected me, but because he could have contracted an STD. So selfish. Between that and all the drug use, you would think he'd be grateful I'm still willing to try. I am merely a convenience. Someone to cook, do his laundry, serve him food, offer sex when he wants it (I don't think he ever considers my needs).

I don't feel treasured, cherished or loved. He doesn't ever buy me anything—it's always the same excuse, I don't have the money. Even when we had money, if he did buy me a gift, it was only at Christmas, when Sarah went with him. I wonder what it would be like to have a husband who cares. Who wanted to teach the kids about God instead of ridiculing me when I do. Someone with whom I could have a pleasant conversation that didn't end up in an argument? What would it be like for my husband to take me out without acting guilty, like we are part of the witness protection. Who would want to go somewhere with me without getting angry or only going begrudgingly on the rare occasion? Who would put God first, then me, and then the kids?

Instead, I'm in last place, along with God; sad, I never thought it would be like this. My children are my most cherished blessing from God, and the best gift from our marriage, and besides the lessons I've learned in the past 30 years, my marriage has been hell. Other couples from church post on FB their love for "their best friend," "who's always there for them," "the love of their life," and I honestly can't relate to that, which breaks my heart. I long for a good relationship with my husband. No matter what I do or say, nothing seems to help. I pray until I don't have breath. Part of me says stick it out. What is my testimony and witness for Christ if I get a divorce? The other part of me says, enough is enough; God doesn't honor drugs, adultery. Brian does not put God first, so why am I wrong to just give up? I'll keep praying.

My stomach hurts most of the time; it's like someone's taken a wire brush to it. I know it's stress. I try not to let things bother me but my stomach isn't listening to my head. For the past four or five days, my blood pressure has been rising and I've had horrible headaches, it feels like my head is ready to pop. Not good! I need to work on this. I pray I can go back to Boeing as it's close to home and I can add to my 23+ years there and support myself. Guess I'd better get some sleep. Woman's Bible Study tomorrow. Don't want to be sleepy for that. I'm really enjoying it.

***End of Thoughts/Journaling

OUR PATHWAY OUT

I still didn't trust Brian. He continued to work through the Union, as well as helping at our church and doing repairs on the side. Time spent at the church was having an impact on him, as was being surrounded by Christians. He started to feel good again about his life. And he had full-time employment through the Union at a good company. That was in May of 2014.

LAURIE KIRBY

SURGERY YET AGAIN

Our daughter Sarah was turning 21 on June 26, 2014. She wanted to take a trip to Yosemite. Brian hadn't been at the new job for long so I would accompany Sarah without him. I booked a cabin in Yosemite for Sarah, her friend Hailey and me. We did a lot of hiking, and the scenery was gorgeous! We had a great time. Shortly after we got back, I began having severe headaches. One day in July, my head felt ready to explode. I thought maybe it was a symptom of perimenopause. I also noticed breast milk appearing and my menstrual cycle was off. I would skip a month or two, have a period that lasted three weeks and was extremely heavy, then no period, and so on. I saw my doctor and he ran a blood test to check my prolactin levels, which were elevated. He then ordered an MRI of my head.

In September 2014, I was diagnosed with a very large pituitary (brain) tumor. When I told Brian and the kids, Brian didn't take it very well, and got high (just that once). Once again, Denny came to the rescue. What he said to Brian really hit home. From that day forward, Brian has been a changed man, and has re-dedicated his life to Christ. That is the only explanation for his transformation.

***

I found a surgeon at UCLA Medical that specialized in treating these types of tumors. I was scheduled to have the tumor removed on November 5, 2014. My sister drove down from Washington to be with our family. I checked into the hospital and was put under anesthesia. UCLA is a teaching hospital, and before the surgery, my MRI scan was projected on a screen overhead and the surgeon described the procedure for the students. It "just so happened" a Radiologist Interventionist, Dr. Nestor Gonzalez was also in the room. (I believe there are no coincidences.) He noticed a bulge by the tumor, which he thought might be an aneurism. I was immediately given a CAT scan with contrast. Sure enough, it was an aneurism. If the aneurism was too large at the base, Dr. Gonzalez would perform a craniotomy (cut away part of the skull to access the brain.) He was hopeful that he could go through the femoral vein. They ordered another type of scan that shows 3D detail of the veins in the brain (so cool, I must say!).

The aneurism coiling was scheduled for December 2, 2014 and the tumor removal for the next day, December 3rd. Dr. Gonzalez was able to go through the femoral artery and coil the aneurism. The following day they performed the tumor removal. The surgeries were successful. The surgeon was able to "peel" off the tumor from the pituitary gland, leaving it intact. At some point, the tumor had "bled out." He asked me if I had experienced any horrific headaches. I mentioned the one I had that previous July. Apparently I had suffered a stroke.

***

God had his Hand in it all. From turning my illness into a spiritual miracle (a return to Christ for Brian), as well as my miraculous medical intervention and spiritual growth, God is always at work in our lives. If I had to go through everything again just to bring Brian back to Christ, I would in a heartbeat. Psalm 103 has a special place in my heart, "Bless the LORD, O MY SOUL: AND ALL THAT IS WITHIN ME, BLESS HIS HOLY NAME. [2] Bless the LORD, O MY SOUL, AND FORGET NOT ALL HIS BENEFITS: [3] Who forgives all thine iniquities; who heals all thy diseases; 4 Who redeemeth thy life from destruction; who crowned thee with lovingkindness and tender mercies; 5 Who satisfies thy mouth with good things; so that thy youth is renewed like the eagle's. [6] The LORD executes righteousness and judgment for all that are oppressed. [7] He made known his ways unto Moses, his acts unto the children of Israel. [8] The LORD IS MERCIFUL AND GRACIOUS, SLOW TO ANGER, AND PLENTEOUS IN MERCY. [9] He will not always chide: neither will he keep his anger forever. [10] He hath not dealt with us after our sins; nor rewarded us according to our iniquities. [11] For as the heaven is high above the earth, so great is his mercy toward them that fear him. [12] As far as the east is from the west, so far hath he removed our transgressions from us. [13] Like as a father pities his children, so the LORD pities them that fear him. [14] For he knows our frame; he remembers that we are dust. [15] As for man, his days are as grass: as a flower of the field, so he flourishes. [16] For the wind passes over it, and it is gone; and the place thereof shall know it no more. [17] But the mercy of the LORD IS FROM EVERLASTING TO EVERLASTING UPON THEM THAT FEAR HIM, AND HIS RIGHTEOUSNESS UNTO CHILDREN'S children; 18 To such as keep his covenant, and to those that remember his commandments to do them. [19] The LORD HATH PREPARED HIS THRONE IN THE HEAVENS; AND HIS KINGDOM rules over all. [20] Bless the LORD, YE HIS ANGELS, THAT EXCEL IN STRENGTH, THAT DO HIS COMMANDMENTS, HEARKENING UNTO THE VOICE OF HIS WORD. [21] Bless ye the LORD, ALL YE HIS HOSTS; YE MINISTERS OF HIS, THAT DO HIS PLEASURE. [22] Bless the LORD, ALL HIS WORKS IN ALL PLACES OF HIS DOMINION: BLESS THE LORD, O MY SOUL."

At my post-op appointment with Dr. Gonzalez, I learned he was able to coil the aneurism and overcome the limitations it posed. I asked if he was a Christian. He said yes, and that was why he knew he could coil the aneurism if the base was large, because God was with him. He prays before each surgery. His ministry is one of prayer for those who experience severe physical illness, especially those who are alone. What a testimony!! Once again, I'm so awed and amazed by God's handprint on my life.

THROUGH IT ALL, OUR GOD

God is a God of love, grace and redemption. I have witnessed this throughout my life, not only in the challenges I faced, but those Brian, and some of my friends, also faced. Sometimes we wonder why we are given trials or illnesses. It may be for our benefit, our spouse's benefit, for our children or even for a stranger. Over the years, many people have told me, "I would never have known you were having a difficult time. You always seemed so happy and full of life." My response is that Christ has been with me in every crisis. I'm also asked how I can believe in a God that would allow so much suffering. My response is, "Maybe it was to give me the spiritual growth and the strength I found in Christ." Others have asked why I didn't file a sexual harassment case. I thought that sharing my faith would be more productive than ruining a man's career. I also knew that at most workplaces if you claim harassment, you will be blackballed, and I had three precious children that depended on me. I want my life to be a reflection of Christ. I want to show I care. I want Christ to shine in every aspect of my life.

GRATITUDE

In April of 2014, I was asked by Nicole Dunaetz to speak at the Women's Tea on Gratitude. My first thought was, "Me? Who am I?" Nicole, being the wise woman she is, probably saw the terror on my face. Ha! She said when interviewing me for a paper she was writing, she was touched by my words of gratitude. After all, I am working on a book about my life and gratitude for what He has done for my family and me.

When she asked me to speak, I was reminded of the story of Moses, when God spoke to him from the burning bush. Moses was asked to demand that Pharaoh release his people. I am certainly not a Moses, but I had the same fear. Moses told God, "Who am I... I can't speak!" He had many excuses, but God was with him. That was me...who am I? Speak in front of all those ladies? Are you sure you have the right lady? Nicole suggested I pray about it, so I did. By the end of Sunday night, I had the answer. How could I not tell of my gratitude? God has done so much for me.

MY CHILDREN

Well, the story doesn't end there. I'm thankful that in the New Covenant (found in Jeremiah, Chapter 31: 29-34), God assures His people that the sins of the fathers will no longer be visited upon their children. Praise God! I take great comfort in this.

Ryan

My eldest son Ryan accepted Christ when he was seven years old. He has earned his AA degree, became a mechanic, and recently bought a townhouse. He knows the Source of his blessings and shares that faith with others.

Sarah

My daughter Sarah is something of a perfectionist. She's always been a good student, and I never had to remind her to do her homework. She was baptized four years ago, and graduated from Cal State Long Beach with a BS degree in Criminal Justice. I know God will lead her to the right job and path in life.

Kyle

Our middle son struggles with drug addiction. He has always been high-spirited, with natural leadership qualities and a big personality. As a child, he had anxiety when I returned to college. After a few weeks of school, I decided not to leave my child for so many hours after work. He feared I would abandon him! He probably thought that since Daddy didn't come home, maybe Mommy wouldn't, either.

My children always came first. I didn't need a college degree to tell me I had value (although my boss was convinced of that). God and my children were my world. I brought my son to a Christian counselor to address these fears. Sometimes he would see her alone and other times it was a joint session. The therapy provided strategies for him to cope with his distress, and gave him a sense of security and stability. It also helped to strengthen our bond.

***

Kyle always had many friends and often invited them to church. So it came as a shock two years ago to learn he had started using drugs. He went to jail, then to state prison, then back to jail, and was released at the end of June 2016 (in for 14 days that time). He seems so lost, searching for direction, although he accepted Christ when he was 12 years old. I tell him he's precious to God and precious to us. And I worry about him, even though he is not "mine," he's God's, and in His hands. He's an adult and must make his own decisions. Just the other day I broke down, asking God why He had allowed Kyle to have this addiction. The new covenant promised the sins of the fathers will no longer be visited upon their children. Why did my child turn to drugs, wasn't it enough that my husband did? Please, Lord, deliver Kyle. Bring him back to you, Lord!!!

***

Redeemed by Grace

Kyle was release then back in jail when we moved to Kentucky at the end of December 2016. During the course of several months, he would call, and Denny O'Keefe would visit him in jail. Something seemed different in him this time; I could see God working on him.

He was due to be released in the middle of August 2017. Brian and I agreed that I needed to be there for his release. I told Kyle he could move to Kentucky to live with us. We believed he needed a fresh start to stay out of trouble. He agreed and was very excited. I drove to California to pick him up from jail. It took five weeks of many prayers and a lot of calling Probation, but finally, we got the "okay" to take Kyle to Kentucky.

Once in Kentucky, we immediately went to the Probation office to sign him up. Kyle started applying for jobs, and within two weeks had one. After only being on probation for a month in Kentucky, they released his probation and said he was done! This was a big weight off of Kyle's shoulders.

He met a girl at work and started casually dating her. She left the company to take another job. After several months, it got more serious. He fell in love with her and her three girls. They all go to church with us. They plan on getting married; not sure of the date yet. Kyle constantly thanks God for all his many blessings and for his redemption.

It's awe inspiring seeing God work before our eyes. How much He loves us to reach down, dust us off, and heap blessing after blessing on us after all we have done. His love knows no bounds. He offers Grace abundantly without holding back. Bring your burdens and thorns to the Lord and leave them there. He wants you to surrender all to Him. Once you surrender all to Him, you can live a life of freedom that only He can provide.

***

I pray for my children, always! I know God hears my prayers and feels my heartbreak. My love for them is immense. I pray for all three of my children to be active in church, serving the Lord. God has a path and plan for them, just as He did for Brian and me. It's painful to see your children going down the wrong path. We all have lessons to learn.

My husband and I still have work to do in our marriage. Having placed our trust in God, we want to share His love with each other, our family, and those around us, those who need the comfort and strength we have found.

MY WISH FOR YOU

I share my journey as a footpath to overcoming the struggles in your life. You may feel like giving up, but never give up!! No sin is too great for God to forgive. God is our Redeemer and can transform us and all our circumstances if we surrender to Him. We are all broken. Only Christ can put the pieces back together.

We each have a story to tell. I pray that you will, "Fight the good fight of faith. Take hold of the eternal life to which you were called when you made your good confession in the presence of many witnesses." 1 Timothy 6:12.

If you have not made a commitment to Christ, I encourage you to do so. Jesus is the hope of our salvation. He will never leave you nor forsake you. His love never fails. He is unchanging and steadfast. God sent His Son Jesus to die for you and me, to forgive us and give us a new life. That's how much He loves us!! Turn to Christ, and rest in knowing that God is in control.

LAURIE KIRBY

ACKNOWLEDGEMENTS

To my family, thank you for loving me and giving me this opportunity to share our lives with others.

To Sharon Chapman, thank you for your love and encouragement to complete this work.

To Denny and Mimi O'Keefe, thank you for your faithful, servant's heart to help those struggling with their marriage and addictions. God has blessed us beyond measure with your friendship and love.

And finally, to Kathleen Marusak, thank you for your friendship, love and editing skills. I cannot tell you how grateful I am that God brought you into my life.

LAURIE KIRBY

ABOUT THE AUTHOR

Because of moving a lot as a child, I always wanted a stable foundation for my family. I found a wonderful church in Oceanside Christian Fellowship, a home for our children in Lakewood, where I passionately pursue people for Christ. My husband and I have moved to Kentucky on a 20-acre farm and desire to be a light in our new community.

"Be Bold for the Lord in All that you do!"
~ Laurie Kirby

LAURIE KIRBY

www.ingramcontent.com/pod-product-compliance
Lightning Source LLC
Chambersburg PA
CBHW060850050426
42453CB00008B/923